Political & Economic Systems

DEMOCRACY

David Downing

H www.heinemann.co.uk/library
Visit our website to find out more information about Heinemann Library books.

To order:
- ☎ Phone 44 (0) 1865 888066
- 📄 Send a fax to 44 (0) 1865 314091
- 💻 Visit the Heinemann Bookshop at www.heinemann.co.uk/library to browse our catalogue and order online.

First published in Great Britain by Heinemann Library, Halley Court, Jordan Hill, Oxford OX2 8EJ, a division of Reed Educational and Professional Publishing Ltd.
Heinemann is a registered trademark of Reed Educational and Professional Publishing Ltd.

OXFORD MELBOURNE AUCKLAND JOHANNESBURG BLANTYRE
GABORONE IBADAN PORTSMOUTH (NH) USA CHICAGO

Designed by AMR
Originated by Dot Gradations
Printed in Hong Kong by South China Printing

ISBN 0 431 12434 5
06 05 04 03 02
10 9 8 7 6 5 4 3 2 1

British Library Cataloguing in Publication Data

Downing, David
  Democracy. – (Political & economic systems)
  1. Democracy – Juvenile literature
  I. Title
  321.8

Acknowledgements
The publishers would like to thank the following for permission to reproduce photographs:
Bridgeman: pp. 12, 20; Bridgeman/British Museum: p. 6; Bridgeman/Lincoln Cathedral: p. 10; Bridgeman/Musee Carnavalet: p. 4; Corbis/Bettmann: p. 32; Corbis/Francis G. Mayer: p. 14; Corbis/Geoffrey Taunton: p. 17; Corbis/Ruggero Vanni: p. 8; Corbis/Sergio Dorantes: p. 47; Corbis/Steve Raymer: p. 31; Corbis/Wally McNamee: p. 43; Corbis/Peter Turnley: p. 53; Hulton Archive: p. 22; PA Photos: p. 29; PA Photos/EPA: pp. 24, 36, 50; PA Photos/EPA Pool Reuters/Jerry Lampen: p. 48; Popperfoto/Apichart Weerawong/Reuters: p. 5; Popperfoto/Danilo Bartulin/Reuters: p. 34; Popperfoto/Eriko Sugita/Reuters: p. 45; Popperfoto/Juda Ngwenya/ Reuters: p. 23; Popperfoto/Paul McErlane/Reuters: p. 37; Popperfoto/Simon Kwong/Reuters: p. 30; Rex/Nils Jorgensen: p. 26; Rex/SIPA Press: p. 38; Stone/Adrian Murrell: p. 41.

Cover photograph: Supporters of Nelson Mandela in the first post-apartheid elections in South Africa, 1994, reproduced with permission of Corbis.

Every effort has been made to contact copyright holders of any material reproduced in this book. Any omissions will be rectified in subsequent printings if notice is given to the publishers.

Our thanks to Christopher Gibb for his comments in the preparation of this book.

◯ Contents

Any words appearing in the text in bold, **like this**, are explained in the glossary.

① Turning points

At the beginning of 1789 France was ruled by King Louis XVI. There was a little-used French **parliament** called the States-General. This included representatives of the three so-called estates or classes (the clergy, the nobility and the common people), but it had no real power.

That summer everything changed. On 17 June the Third Estate, representing the common people, declared itself a new National Assembly. Three days later, locked out of their usual meeting hall, the representatives met in an indoor tennis court, where they signed an oath to stay together until France had a **constitution** based on the will of the people.

The meeting in the Parisian tennis court, as painted by the famous French artist Jaques-Louis David.

The King tried to reassert his authority, but on 14 July a mob stormed one of his prisons in Paris – the Bastille – and he was forced to withdraw his troops from the city. In the weeks that followed, the new National Assembly abolished the social and economic system, divided the country into *départments* ruled by elected assemblies, and drew up a Declaration of Rights. This said that **sovereignty**, or power, lay not with the monarch but with the people.

France had crossed the line which separates **dictatorship** from democracy.

The events of that summer were an important turning point in the long history of democracy. There have been many others. The French Third Estate had been influenced by the American Revolution a decade earlier, and throughout the next century, people struggling for democratic rights would find inspiration in both these revolutions. The 20th century opened with the ferocious struggle to win the vote for women in Britain; as the century drew to a close, the nations of eastern Europe celebrated their release from **communism**. Millions watched on TV as Nelson Mandela walked away from prison, victorious in the long struggle to create democracy in South Africa.

FOR DETAILS ON KEY PEOPLE, SEE PAGES 59–60.

It has not all been one-way traffic, of course. The murder of pro-democracy protesters in Beijing's Tiananmen Square in June 1989 was also shown around the world. There has been no shortage of men and women prepared to suffer imprisonment and worse, rather than submit to dictatorial governments. As the 21st century began, many brave campaigners for democracy in their countries – Burma's Aung San Suu Kyi is a good example – remained under arrest.

Aung San Suu Kyi, the leader of the Burmese pro-democracy movement, greeting supporters outside her house in July 1995.

② An idea in waiting

Imagine a group of prehistoric men gathered round an evening fire, discussing the question of where they would hunt on the following day. These are the tribe's older, more experienced hunters, and they feel more or less equally qualified to put forward their point of view and have it listened to. Here by their fire, these men are taking part in a democratic process, not because they like the idea of democracy, but because it seems common sense to make use of everyone's experience.

Greek democracy

Small independent groups like this, and the sense of natural equality which flourished within them, eventually fell victim to the larger communities which accompanied the spread of agriculture and permanent settlements. In these communities, power was not shared so equally, and there was no place for democracy. For several thousand years most societies were ruled by **monarchies**, **dictators** or small groups of individuals (oligarchies).

Democracy, the process of involving citizens in government, resurfaced in several city-states in what is now Greece around the end of the 6th century BC, and it was probably the citizens of Athens who coined the word *demokratia* (democracy) – a combination of *demos* (the people) and *kratos* (to rule) – to describe their system of government.

A marble statue of the Athenian leader Pericles, an early champion of democracy.

The central feature of this system was the Assembly, a regular mass meeting at which those who were considered citizens could have their say. The Assembly elected ten generals to run the military, but the ruling council of 500 members (the Boule) and other public officers were picked out by a lottery in which all citizens had an equal chance. Since those chosen could only serve for a limited period, every citizen had a good chance of being selected at least once in his lifetime.

Other citizens' rights were necessary for the system to work as it was supposed to. The most important of these was free speech, without which there could be no real debate in either the Assembly or the Boule.

Early limits to democracy

There were definite limits to the sort of democracy which was practised in Athens and other Greek city-states, limits which would also apply to many democratic systems right down to the present day. The franchise, or right to vote, was given to all *citizens*, but not to all adults. Women, slaves and foreigners were not considered citizens, and therefore only a quarter of the adult population actually took part in the democratic process. Also, the rich continued to have ways of influencing events which were not available to the poor (bribing elected officials, for example), regardless of how equal they were supposed to be as citizens.

The importance of free debate

'Our ordinary citizens, though occupied with the pursuits of industry, are still fair judges of public matters ... And instead of looking on discussion as a stumbling-block in the way of action, we think it an indispensable preliminary to any wise action at all.'

(Athenian politician Pericles, explaining in 431 BC how important free discussion was to reaching the right decisions)

FOR DETAILS ON KEY PEOPLE, SEE PAGES 59–60.

Even this limited democracy worried famous **philosophers** such as Socrates, Plato and Aristotle, all of whom feared that the poor were too stupid or irrational to be given such responsibility! They preferred the idea of rule by the wise and the politically skilled, by men who knew what the people wanted better than the people themselves. The thinkers of the time believed that well-meaning but decidedly undemocratic governments should act as parents or guardians, acting in their people's best interests whether they wanted them to or not. This idea has lingered on through the centuries.

The Roman Republic

Greek democracy lasted only a few hundred years, finally dying out around the 2nd century BC. During this same period, the Roman Republic also flourished, and while not a democracy in the Greek sense, it had democratic characteristics. After an early period in which only the aristocrats – men who had inherited positions of power – took part in government, the common people were allowed to hold some offices and elect their own leader.

The ruins of the Roman Forum, where democratic assemblies were held in the years of the Roman Republic.

When the Romans began to conquer other lands, the newly conquered people were allowed to become Roman citizens and share in these democratic practices – or at least that was the idea. In reality, the expansion of Roman rule over such a vast expanse of territory made it impossible for most of these citizens to have any influence on the government, which remained in Rome. The idea of sending representatives from the regions to the capital never caught on.

By the last century BC, the Republic's democratic institutions had been destroyed by corrupt officials and power-hungry soldiers, and the Republic itself replaced by a dictatorial Empire. For the next 600 years, democracy virtually disappeared.

New assemblies

Democracy reappeared in northern Europe around AD 600. In order to settle disputes and discuss new laws for their communities, groups of Vikings would call an assembly or Thing. They were not inspired by memories of Greek or Roman democracy – they had probably never heard of it – but were simply acting as people who regarded each other as equals.

Around AD 930 the Vikings on Iceland created the Althing, an assembly for the whole island, which lasted for more than three centuries. Over the next 500 years similar regional and national assemblies came into being throughout Scandinavia. Similar bodies also made their first appearances in the Low Countries and England, but here the principle of equality only played a small role in their creation. The expansion of manufacturing and trade had seen the rise of a new and wealthy business class, and the traditional rulers of these countries – usually **monarchs** of one sort or another – were often in dire need of money.

As the centuries went by, these rulers, rather than risk provoking violent opposition by simply taking what they wanted, often chose instead to summon an assembly of the rich and powerful. These people would then decide how to arrange things in both their own and the monarch's interest. In their early years such assemblies represented only one small section of society, but during the centuries that followed an increasing proportion of the population would, for a variety of reasons, be allowed to take part.

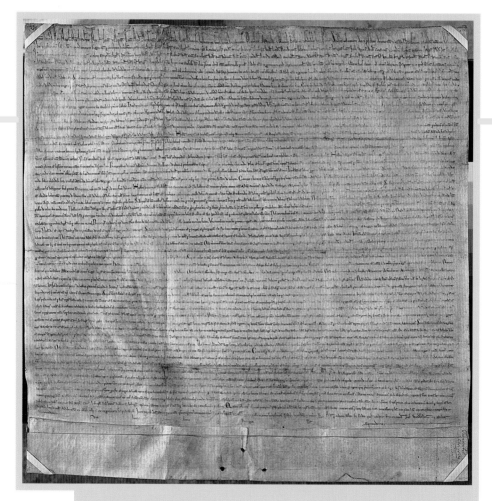

A copy of the English Magna Carta (Great Charter), the document limiting the powers of the monarchy which King John was forced to sign at Runnymede in 1215.

The British Parliament

The most famous of these assemblies, and the one that would most influence the development of democracy, was the British Parliament. This came to have two chambers, or Houses. The original band of rich and powerful **nobles** which the monarch consulted grew into the **House of Lords**. The representatives of the property-owning middle class were elected by the people, into what became the House of Commons, which soon developed into the more powerful of the two chambers. Separately and together these Houses slowly managed to limit the authority of the monarch, until the system reached what seemed a natural balance of power and a natural division of tasks. Roughly speaking, Parliament proposed new measures and laws (the **legislative** function of government) and the monarch made sure that they were carried out (the **executive** function). Independent judges interpreted the laws when necessary (the **judicial** function). Each of these three powers was a check on the other two.

This system was not set up in response to a popular demand for democracy. It was simply the way in which the various groups at the top of the society arranged to share power. However, those who wished to expand representation beyond the upper classes – and to further limit the powers of the monarch, who represented no one but his or herself – were happy to call themselves supporters of greater democracy. The ideal itself was further strengthened by the rise of **Protestantism**. If, as some Protestants came to claim, all humans were equal in God's eyes, then surely they should also be equal when it came to choosing and running governments.

In Britain, these threads came together in the 17th century. A stubborn king – Charles I – tried to reduce the power of Parliament, and plunged the country into a **civil war** which cost him his throne and his life. He was beheaded in 1649. In the process the idea of a democracy which involved all the people was given a huge boost. One particular group – the Levellers – made some startling suggestions. They argued that all men should have an equal vote in annual elections, that those elected should carry out the people's instructions rather than think for themselves, and that members of parliament should serve only two terms in a row. Such proposals, though perhaps impractical, were very much in tune with the spirit of the long-vanished Greek democracy.

The Putney debates

In October and November of 1647 the victors in the English Civil War held a series of political debates at Putney, outside London. One of the Levellers, Colonel Rainsborough, argued for universal male suffrage (right to vote). 'I think it's clear, that every man that is to live under a government', he said, 'ought first by his own consent to put himself under that government.' The more conservative General Ireton disagreed. He thought the vote should be restricted to those who had property.

King Charles I entering the House of Commons to arrest five Members of Parliament in January 1642. They had already flown. Civil war between King and Parliament broke out three months later.

The Levellers were defeated, and the monarchy restored in 1660. The new deal which was struck between Parliament and the monarchy – the so-called Glorious Revolution of 1688 – effectively locked the common people out of the political process. By this time many other countries had assemblies or parliaments, but, as in England, fewer than 5 per cent of the population were allowed to vote. All these assemblies either lacked any real power or were entirely composed of the rich and privileged.

Most of the rich and privileged, like the Greek philosophers of old, imagined that democracy was just another word for mob rule, and did everything they could to oppose it. Most ordinary people accepted this state of affairs; there was little popular demand for increased participation in the political process. As the 18th century unfolded, there was little sign of the democratic revolutions to come.

Some political thinkers

In the 17th and 18th centuries several influential studies of government were written in Britain and France. The most important of these were John Locke's *Two Treatises of Government* (1690), the Baron de Montesquieu's *The Spirit of the Laws* (1748) and Jean-Jacques Rousseau's *The Social Contract* (1762). Each, in their different ways, recommended greater democracy, and each would influence many of those involved in the American and French revolutions.

③ Representative democracy

In the last quarter of the 18th century, revolutions in British colonies in America (1775–76) and in France (1789–94) placed the idea of democracy at the centre of the world stage. Both revolutions erupted in response to what was seen as **tyranny**. Both claimed the right of the mass of the people to choose a different government to the one they had. The American colonists, who felt that they were paying taxes to a state which allowed them no say in its decisions, coined the phrase 'no taxation without representation'. The Declaration of Independence they signed in 1776 emphasized that governments only held just powers by the consent (agreement) of the governed. In France the Declaration of Rights proclaimed that the source of all **sovereignty** lies essentially in the nation. By the standards of the time, these were deeply democratic revolutions.

Leaders of Britain's American colonies sign the American Declaration of Independence.

Having swept aside the previous systems of rule, the victorious revolutionaries set out to devise new, democratic systems to put in their place. This was not a simple task, or a straightforward one. The American and French revolutionaries had many important decisions to make. These decisions would determine how user-friendly, long-lasting and democratic, their democracies would be.

How representative?

Since there was no chance of getting the entire adult male populations of either France or the new USA into a city square, the direct democracy which had flourished in the Greek city-states, where matters were discussed and decisions taken by all involved, was clearly out of the question. The new systems would have be **representative democracies**, in which the mass of the people would elect a few of their number to represent their views in the new assemblies.

This shift from direct democracy to representative democracy was considered inevitable by everyone, but some political thinkers still worried that democracy would be damaged in the process. Democracy, after all, was about bridging the gap between governments and governed – might not a new gap open between the people and their representatives?

British thinkers such as Tom Paine (who was very influential in the USA) and James Mill suggested frequent elections to prevent the representatives growing away from the people. Paine and Mill argued that if representatives had to keep putting themselves forward for election, then they were more likely to listen to what the electors had to say. Like the Levellers, they believed that representatives should only serve a limited number of terms.

What did representing a group of people actually mean? Was the representative supposed simply to follow the instructions of the majority who voted for him? Or was he expected to use his own judgement? If the latter, then how far could his judgement differ from that of the people whom he was supposed to represent? What worried people like Paine and Mill was the possibility that free representatives, unhindered by frequent elections, limited terms or obedience to their electors' wishes, would eventually form themselves into a permanent political class with its own interests, separate from those of the people.

Others, like Edmund Burke in Britain and Alexander Hamilton in the USA, disagreed. They liked the fact that representative democracy placed a gap between government and people, that it allowed the well-educated and well-informed representatives to make the decisions, rather than the poorly educated and poorly informed common people. This gap prevented democracy from turning into the mob rule they feared; it allowed the creation of a political class which could rule wisely on the people's behalf, a development which they warmly welcomed.

The inevitable answer

'Since all cannot, in a community exceeding a single small town, participate personally in any but some very minor portions of the public business, it follows that the ideal type of a perfect government must be representative.'

(English political thinker John Stuart Mill, the son of James Mill, writing in 1861)

A political class

The tension between these two groups has continued to this day. One is ever pushing for greater democracy, the other is striving to keep democracy within what it considers sensible limits. Generally speaking, those who wished to limit democracy have had their way. Elections are usually held at intervals of between

A statue of John Stuart Mill in London's Temple Gardens. Like his father, James Mill, J.S. Mill was an influential UK political thinker.

four and seven years, which seems over-long to those who want more popular influence over decision-making, and more democratic accountability. The number of terms a representative can serve are rarely limited, with the notable exception of the US president, who since 1951 has only been allowed two terms in office.

In most countries representatives have indeed formed themselves into a political class, which is usually divided among two or more political parties. This political class – or political elite, as it is sometimes called – needs to take note of popular desires, particularly around election times, but it tends to be the political class, rather than the people, who decide what will be discussed and voted on. Each party devises and offers a package of programmes which it thinks the electorate (those with the vote) will find appealing. The one which wins the most votes or seats in the relevant assemblies gets the chance to put into effect as many of those programmes as it then wishes. This is representative democracy of a sort, but falls some way short of the model favoured by people like Tom Paine and James Mill.

④ Constitutions and the franchise

Setting up a **representative democracy** involves a lot more than simply electing a **legislative assembly** to debate new measures and laws. How will the executive – the branch of government which puts these new measures and policies into practice – be chosen? How will the three-way relationship between **legislative**, **executive**, and **judiciary** work? How much power will this central government have over administrations functioning at the lower levels of state, province or city? Each nation's answers to these questions are set out in its **constitution** – the way its particular political system is constituted, or set up.

The British system

The British political system evolved gradually over a millennium, and bore the marks of the monarchy's long losing struggle with **Parliament**. In the 17th century the elected body first took over the legislative powers, leaving the monarch to function as the executive arm of government; in the 18th century the monarch was forced to hand over much of this remaining power to a prime (first) minister. By the 19th century the monarch's role was almost entirely symbolic.

Sovereignty now rested in Parliament, which elected its own executive arm or government. This was headed by a prime minister, who appointed ministers to head the various government departments. Since the UK is a relatively small country there was, at least until recently, little pressure for strong regional rule, so a unitary system rather than a **federal** one was adopted. In a unitary system, the central government was always sure of having the final say.

The fact that the British system was not built to specifications, but simply evolved over time, has left it with certain features which appear either old-fashioned or undemocratic, or both.

There is no written constitution, no written statement (bill of people's rights), and the monarchy retains some power, at least in theory. Neither judges nor the second chamber are elected, although the ongoing reform of the latter may eventually involve election of some members. The executive must be trusted not to abuse the powers it holds.

The American system

The Americans who set out to frame a constitution for the USA in the years after their revolution were keen to take on board, and if possible improve upon, the better parts of the British system. They were also determined to cast the worst parts overboard. In particular, they had no desire to create their own monarchy. They decided instead on a republic, with a separately elected executive **presidency**.

Declaration of democracy

'We hold these truths to be self-evident, that all men are created equal, that they are endowed by their Creator with certain inalienable Rights [rights that cannot be taken away], that among these are Life, Liberty and the pursuit of Happiness. That to secure these rights, Governments are instituted [set up] among Men, deriving their just powers from the consent of the governed.'

(The beginning of the American Declaration of Independence (1776). It was written by Thomas Jefferson, who later served as Secretary of State, Vice-President and President.)

One of these constitution-makers, the future President Thomas Jefferson, was keen to create a system in which the various arms – the legislative Congress, the executive presidency and the judiciary (headed by the Supreme Court, whose members are appointed but not politically **acccountable**) – would act as checks and balances on each other's power. This separation of powers would prevent any of the three branches of government from abusing its power.

FOR DETAILS ON KEY PEOPLE, SEE PAGES 59–60.

This system was built to specifications; it was written down, and it did include a bill of rights. The huge geographical size of the USA, and the deep divisions in interests, outlook and culture which characterized the different regions, meant that a federal system, one in which each of the states of the Union retained significant powers, was considered appropriate. In the event of a dispute between the two levels of government – as, for example, when certain Southern states refused to implement federal laws banning racial segregation – the Supreme Court would be asked to decide for one side or the other.

Thomas Jefferson, who wrote the American Declaration of Independence and later served as President of the United States (1801–9).

These two systems – British parliamentary democracy and American presidential democracy – have both stood the test of time. Each works in its own way, and both have been much imitated over the last 200 years. Other countries have introduced variations on the two themes, sometimes combining what they see as the best features of each, sometimes leaving out those elements which they think are no longer relevant. All the Scandinavian countries, for example, have done away with the second or upper chambers which both the UK (the **House of Lords**) and the USA (the Senate) retain. Other countries have added a bill on social and economic rights to existing bills of political rights.

Expanding the right to vote

The other great issue which faced the revolutionaries of the late 18th century, one which has continued to provoke heated debate and violent struggles ever since, was the extent of the franchise – the number of those who had the right to vote. These days we tend to assume that all adults should have the vote, but this was far from clear to those who took part in the American and French revolutions.

The **French Revolution** initially offered the vote only to people with a certain amount of property, and a decision in 1793 to introduce universal male suffrage (votes for all adult men) was never brought into use. Many Americans also wanted universal male suffrage, but those who wrote the new constitution, keen to protect the interests of the rich and powerful, insisted on a property restriction. More Americans owned property than was the case in Europe, but some 40 per cent of adult white males were still denied the vote. Women and slaves were excluded as a matter of course, and it would be the late 1960s before many descendants of the slaves were actually able to exercise a right to vote.

A UK campaigner for women's right to vote clings to the railings of Buckingham Palace in an effort to resist arrest.

Through the 19th century the franchise in the most developed countries was widened at regular intervals – in the UK, for example, the percentage of adult males entitled to vote rose in several steps from 5 per cent in 1831 to 100 per cent in 1918 – but each new advance was met with opposition. The upper and middle classes' fear of mob rule, of working-class domination through sheer numbers, was slow to fade, and philosophers such as the Englishman John Stuart Mill argued that rule by the mass of ordinary people posed a terrible threat to individual liberty. He suggested that elections should be less frequent, and that better-educated people should have more votes.

In the developed world of North America and north-western Europe these arguments were finally lost early in the 20th century. In these parts of the world most countries had adopted universal male suffrage (votes for all men) by the beginning of World War I, universal female suffrage by the beginning of World War II.

By the middle of the 20th century, in the richer and most powerful countries of the West, rich and poor alike had come to consider democracy the only truly acceptable form of government, and other countries were encouraged to follow their example. Towards the end of the 20th century, the collapse of both European **communism** and South African **apartheid** were seen as further important steps along the road to a democratic world.

When women over the age of 21 got the vote

New Zealand	1893
Australia	1902
Finland	1906
Russia	1917
Canada	1918
Germany	1919
USA	1920
Britain	1928
France	1944

Black South Africans queuing to vote for the first time, April 1994.

⑤ Voting

Voting (or casting one's vote) has always been a central feature of any democratic system. In ancient Greece it was done by a show of hands, a method which is still used today in many meetings. In modern politics, however, where even a minor local election involves thousands of people, votes are cast at an officially supervised polling (voting) station. The details of the procedure vary from country to country, but typically the voters put a mark against the name or names of those they wish to represent them, and place their completed voting or ballot papers through a slot in a sealed container. In the USA, machines are commonly used, with voters punching cards to register their choices.

Most countries with a long experience of democracy operate a **secret ballot**. The names of voters are checked by officials, but their names do not appear on the ballot papers, so no one actually knows who voted for whom. This secrecy was enforced – in Australia in 1856, Britain in 1872, the USA in 1884 – because an open ballot meant that people could be pressured into voting against their own interests by those, like their landlords or employers, who had power over them.

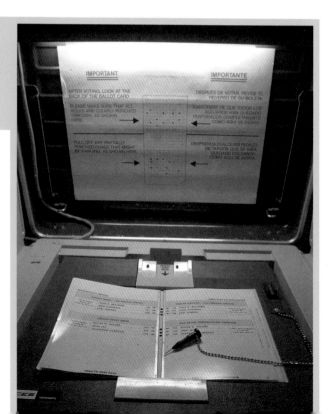

Inside a US voting booth.

Political parties

In most cases people vote for an individual who represents a political party. Individuals can still stand for election in their own right, but since the 18th century the dominance of the political parties has become increasingly overwhelming.

Where did parties come from? Essentially, people who agreed with each other on the main issues of the day joined together for practical reasons. As well-organized groups they were much better equipped to raise money, fight elections, and operate in the elected assemblies, whether as a government or an opposition.

Like representative democracy itself, parties were necessary for democracy to work in a large modern society. In most cases, individuals could join the political party of their choice, attend local meetings and national conferences, and become fully involved in debating, deciding and promoting those ideas and policies which their party would then offer to the wider electorate.

What have parties stood for? Often, they have reflected the interests of economic groups or classes. The Labour Party in the UK, for example, was formed in the 1890s to represent the interests of the British working class, and for more than half a century it promoted policies which it believed would support and defend those working-class

Referendums

In some democratic systems, some decisions – particularly those which involve changing the country's **constitution** – are thought too important to leave to **representative democracy**. Instead, rather in the manner of ancient Greece, the people as a whole are given a direct vote. Such votes are called referendums (or sometimes plebiscites), and are usually decided by a simple majority. The British people, for example, were asked in 1973 to vote in a referendum on whether or not the UK should join the European Economic Community (they voted yes).

25

interests. In the 1930s the Democratic Party in the USA had similar policies.

These parties were considered left of centre on the political spectrum. Those major parties who opposed them at that time – the Conservatives in the UK, the Republicans in the USA – were considered right of centre because, among other things, they were more pro-business, more opposed to government intervention in the economy, and more inclined to place individual freedom before the needs of the community.

The terms 'left' and 'right' have traditionally offered a rough guide to where parties stand on a whole range of important issues. Democracy is not one of these issues. Parties of both left and right have been both democratic and undemocratic.

The annual conference of the British Labour Party. In Britain all the major parties hold such conferences to discuss their policies. They usually take place over several days and involve hundreds of delegates from all over the country.

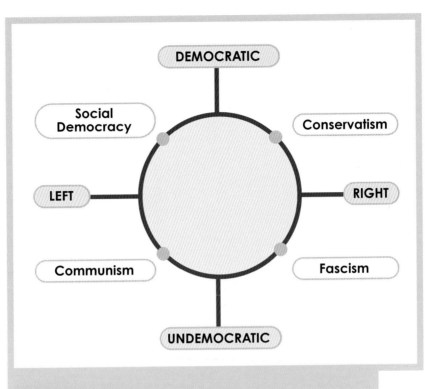

The 'circle of political beliefs', which shows that attitudes towards democracy can differ widely among those of both the 'left' and the 'right'.

Electoral systems

Organizing a system of voting is also far from straightforward, and many different systems have been devised over the years. All of them involve voting in a particular area – a Congressional district in the USA, a parliamentary constituency in the UK or France – but there the similarities end. In some cases, one representative is elected from the area; in others, two or more from a list. In some cases, a representative needs to win more votes than any other single candidate. In other cases, a representative must win more than 50 per cent of the vote, either in the original election or in a second election against the original runner-up.

27

There are many variations of electoral systems, but only two main types. In the first past the post (FPTP) system, which is used in both US and British general elections, the candidate who wins the most votes in his or her electoral district is elected. This means that if Party A received 51 per cent of the votes in each district then it would win 100 per cent of the seats in the assembly; if Party B got 49 per cent of the votes in each district it would receive no seats at all. In such circumstances, the composition (make-up) of the elected congress or parliament would obviously not reflect the opinions of the people.

Fortunately for FPTP, regional differences in wealth, traditional party support and many other factors mean that opinions are never spread that evenly. However, FPTP does produce exaggerated majorities. In the election in the UK in 2001, the Labour Party secured a landslide (overwhelming) victory with fewer than 40 per cent of the votes actually cast. FPTP also works against smaller parties – the UK Green Party, for example – which may be popular throughout the country but cannot manage a winning level of support in any particular constituency.

The other major type of electoral system, widely used in continental Europe, is **proportional representation**, or PR. This can be set up in a number of different ways, but the main point is to ensure that the number of votes cast fully reflects the number of assembly seats won. One way of doing this is by creating electoral districts with a higher number of representatives – say, ten.

Electing a US president

In the United States, presidents are elected by a two-stage process. People in each state vote for a presidential candidate. They also vote for a number of electors to send to a national electoral college (assembly). The members of this college then formally elect the president by voting for the candidate with the highest popular vote in their state. The 2000 election between George W. Bush and Al Gore showed that it is possible under this system for a candidate (Gore) to win a majority of the nationwide vote yet fail to secure a winning majority in the electoral college.

Each party will make up a list of ten candidates, and if, for example, a particular party wins 30 per cent of the vote, then the top three names on their list will be elected.

After the votes have been counted a victorious candidate – in this case the former actress Glenda Jackson (Labour) – celebrates her election to the British Parliament.

Since, in such a situation, a party would only need 10 per cent of the votes to have a representative elected, PR tends to boost the number of parties with a chance of power. This certainly allows more views to be expressed, but those who favour FPTP argue that PR also has significant flaws. Voters can elect representatives who reflect their views more accurately, but these representatives then have to do deals with other parties, which hold diferent views, to form a government. Since these governments are formed of people who disagree with each other they tend to be weak, short-lived or both.

Supporters of PR reply that whatever its weaknesses, their system reflects the actual will of the people better, and is therefore more democratic.

⑥ The crucial ingredients

When **communist** parties were in power in eastern Europe (1947–89), elections were held on a regular basis. Voters were allowed to take part in a secret ballot to choose between candidates for local and national assemblies. In some countries these candidates even represented different political parties. Were these countries – which called themselves 'people's democracies' – truly democratic?

The answer is no. These communist countries had set up a democratic system, but they had refused to provide the people with the other ingredients needed to make the system work in a democratic way.

Free elections and freedoms

The first such ingredients are fair elections. Elections must offer voters a real choice between parties offering different programmes. They must be supervised by elected officials who have no vested interest in who wins or loses, who can be trusted to make sure that no one votes more than once and that votes are honestly and accurately counted. This was rarely the case in the communist countries of eastern Europe, and cannot always be taken for granted in even the more developed countries of the West, as was demonstrated in Florida during the US **presidential** election in the year 2000.

A demonstrator for freedom of speech in Taipei, the capital of Taiwan, May 1999.

A second group of even more fundamental ingredients are those freedoms – of expression, assembly, association, and the media (newspapers, radio and TV) – which allow democracy to function. These freedoms provide the oxygen which democracy needs to breathe. So what are they? Freedom of expression allows issues to be debated, governments to be criticized and alternatives proposed. Freedom of assembly permits people to gather for such discussions. Freedom of association allows them to join together in parties or pressure groups to get their views across. These three freedoms make it possible for the people to join in the democratic process.

Freedom of the media – that is, media not run by the government in power – should provide the information people need to make their own democratic choices. Without free media, and without the wider freedom of expression (in conversation, books, films, even wall-posters), it is often hard for people to know what is actually happening, and even harder for them to make informed decisions about how they should best vote to achieve the society they desire.

A range of newspapers for sale in a Western democracy. For a democracy to work well, people must have access to a wide range of opinions.

Freedom of speech

'If all mankind, minus one, were of one opinion, and only one person were of the contrary opinion, mankind would be no more justified in silencing that one person, than he, if he had the power, would be justified in silencing mankind.'

(From John Stuart Mill's book *On Liberty*, published in 1859)

The rule of law

Another crucial ingredient, which is often taken for granted in those countries with a long tradition of democracy, is the **rule of law**. It is no good a government allowing all the above freedoms to flourish if it is prepared to override them at moments of crisis. In China in 1957 the communist leader Mao Zedong encouraged the people to speak out with the slogan 'Let a hundred flowers bloom, let a hundred schools of thought contend [do battle with each other]'. There was so much criticism of the government that the experiment was soon stopped, and many critics found themselves in jail. Most seriously of all, it made the Chinese people rightfully afraid to criticize their leaders, even when encouraged to do so. For the freedoms to flourish, people must trust in their permanency, and they can only do that when those who have the job of upholding them – the judges and police, in particular – cannot be pressured by governments into setting them aside.

Beijing's 'Democracy Wall' in April 1980. Local residents read a nine-page poster denouncing a new clampdown on China's pro-democracy movement.

No perfect scores

None of the ingredients listed above were present to any significant degree in the so-called people's democracies of eastern Europe. Individual freedoms were limited, the media heavily

The rule of law

'Wherever law ends, tyranny begins.'

(The English political philosopher John Locke, emphasizing, in his *Two Treatises on Government*, that the rule of law is essential to democracy)

restricted and the rule of law operated only at the communist party's convenience. The new governments which have emerged in those countries are in most cases more democratic. They have joined that process of global democratization which has been proceeding in fits and starts for several centuries, but they cannot be expected to become fully democratic overnight. Even those countries which have been improving their democratic institutions for two centuries are still some way short of that.

In these latter countries, with occasional exceptions, the rule of law operates, individual freedoms are upheld, and elections are conducted fairly. That said, there has often been very little to choose between the major parties. In the USA and the UK, for example, recent elections have usually been contested by two major parties committed to the defence of a free enterprise society with limited government intervention in the economy.

This lack of choice has not been challenged by the mass media. The newspapers, radio and TV stations, though largely free of government control or interference, are mostly owned by the rich and powerful, who share the main parties' interest in opposing far-reaching change. Democracy works in these countries, but far from perfectly.

⑦ Fertile soil, stony ground

Democracy is not like an old-style electric light, either off or on. It is like a light with a dimmer switch. It can certainly be turned off, but it can also shine at varying degrees of brightness. The crucial ingredients discussed in the last chapter (free and fair elections; the freedoms of expression, assembly and association; the **rule of law**) must be present, at least to some degree, for the light to shine at all, but there are several other important factors which can cause it to fade or brightly blaze.

Physical threats

One vital consideration is the presence or absence of a direct physical threat to the democratic system. Such a threat can come from inside or outside the country, from the overwhelming political, economic or military might of other states or the country's own armed forces and police.

The history of the 20th century was sadly littered with examples of large states undermining or destroying the democracies of smaller ones. The USA intervened on many occasions in the affairs of Latin America.

Chile's democratically elected communist president, Salvador Allende (third from right), during the military coup which led to his overthrow and death in September 1973.

The USA played a large role in overthrowing the democratically elected governments of Guatemala in 1954 and Chile in 1973, and replacing them with pro-US military **dictatorships**. Throughout the **Cold War** period, the threat of Soviet military intervention hung over neighbouring eastern Europe, and when any democratic activity took place – as in Czechoslovakia in 1968 – Soviet tanks were sent in to crush it.

Other countries, particularly in the **developing world**, have faced a similar threat from their own military forces. In Nigeria, for example, the attempt to create a working democratic system has been continually interrupted by military takeovers. Here and elsewhere the motives behind such takeovers are mixed: sometimes a simple lust for power, at other times a desire to stamp out the **corruption** which a young and inexperienced democracy has encouraged. Whatever the motives, democracy cannot be expected to thrive when the country's army is effectively holding a gun to its head. In a democratic system the military must always be under the control of the elected government.

No coincidence

The central American country of Costa Rica has not had any armed forces since 1949. It is also the only country in Latin America which has maintained a continuous record of democratic government since World War II.

A democratic culture

The belief that the military should be subject to civilian control is deeply ingrained in older democratic countries such as the UK and the USA. It is part of the democratic culture – that set of beliefs held by the vast majority of the population which supports democracy.

Put simply, the people of these countries believe that the only acceptable way of doing things is the democratic way. They are not recent converts to the idea. They have inherited a long tradition of democratic thought and practice. It would take a crisis of enormous dimensions, a complete breakdown of the way the current society operates, to make people question this democratic tradition and the way they live and govern themselves. The democratic culture in such countries is strong.

General Sani Abacha, leader of Nigeria's military government, inspecting a guard of honour in 1996. Nigeria has since returned to civilian rule.

In other countries, of course, democratic culture is weaker or even non-existent. When various political and economic crises erupted between World Wars I and II, Italy and Germany, whose democratic culture was still very young, soon gave in to the argument that a strong dictatorship was needed to put things right.

Today, there are still countries, such as China, which have no historical experience of democratic rule. Even if democratic institutions are introduced in such places, a democratic culture will need decades to establish itself.

It is also worth bearing in mind here that democracy means the rule of the people, not simply the rule of the majority. Governments, of course, are usually run by the party which has won the most votes, but in a truly democratic culture they must also take note of the wishes of the minority. In Northern Ireland, for example, the **Protestant** community has always been in the majority. Most outsiders now accept that over the years it has often used this dominant position to keep the minority Catholic population from having any say in the way the province is run. Without a strong democratic culture, democracy can easily degenerate into the **tyranny** of the majority.

In October 2000, a woman walks past a mural glorifying the Protestant paramilitary group, the Ulster Freedom Fighters, in Belfast's Shankill road.

Shared values

It is usually easier for one group of people to accept the opinions of another group if both groups share the same basic values. In a similar way, in countries with a population who share values, culture and ethnic background, it is often easier for people to accept those governments which they have not actually voted for. Democracy is not seen as a possible threat because everyone in the country shares and accepts the same way of life. Until recently at least, this situation existed in most European countries.

If countries are divided between ethnic, religious or linguistic (language) groups, and basic values are not shared, then there may be problems. Democracy is built around the idea of compromise, of accepting that sometimes we don't get the government or the policies we want. However, people are often unwilling to compromise when it comes to their most basic values.

Elizabeth Rehn, UN special reporter for human rights in Bosnia, visits a field outside Srebrenica which is littered with the remains of Muslim refugees slaughtered by Serbs in July 1995. The various cultures in Bosnia found it impossible to settle their differences peacefully or democratically.

If members of a large minority culture feel that their interests are being ignored or opposed by members of a majority culture, then that minority may decrease its support for the country's democratic system.

There are ways of getting round such problems. The USA, at least until recently, successfully persuaded immigrants from a variety of cultures to adopt a new set of shared American values. Countries divided along ethnic or national lines like Belgium and Switzerland have set up their democratic systems in particular ways – adopting **proportional representation (PR)**, allowing each national community a **veto** (right to reject a proposal) in certain circumstances – which make it almost impossible for any one culture to dominate the others. In some cases, a **federal constitution** has provided minorities with additional protection; in others, autonomous status (having some powers of self-government) has provided minorities with the right to take at least some decisions for themselves.

In the last resort minority cultures can decide that no such compromises are possible, and seek to set up countries of their own. Such attempts sometimes succeed (the creation of Slovakia, for example, following the break-up of Czechoslovakia in 1993), but often they are successfully opposed, as when the Southern states of the USA attempted to leave the Union in 1861.

A lack of other options

Fascism offered aggression, racism and an economy which relied on producing arms. **Communism** sacrificed democracy in return for centrally planned economic growth, and ended up with neither. Military and other dictatorships after World War II have been brutal and unsuccessful. Those who believe in democracy can argue that, for all its failings in practice, it still seems far better than any of the alternatives on display in the 20th century.

A measure of equality

In a democracy all citizens are supposed to have equal political rights: the same number of votes, the same right to stand for election, the same access to information. No one should have more influence on the decision-making process than anyone else.

Unfortunately, this political equality is often weakened by economic inequality. Even in the longest-established democratic systems, the rich can buy favours from the parties with their financial contributions, decide what will be discussed, and influence debate through their ownership of the media. In younger, less well-established democratic systems, the scope for bribery and **corruption** is usually much higher, because people are not so used to honest behaviour in politics.

When the French historian Alexis de Tocqueville wrote his famous book *Democracy in America* in the mid-19th century, he made the point that the gap between rich and poor was, at that time, much narrower in the USA than it was in Europe. This social and economic equality was, he thought, the reason why US democracy was doing so well.

The market economy

Democratic conditions have only ever existed for any length of time in countries with **capitalist** or **market economies**, those in which most property is privately owned and in which most goods are bought and sold in a free market place. This supports the widely held view that such economies create favourable conditions for democracy. However, those same market economies also create conditions which can limit democracy.

Market economies have proved themselves more efficient at producing growth than any of the alternatives. Societies which can afford to share the wealth around are usually more tolerant, more inclined to accept those compromises which make democracy possible.

Such economies produce strong middle classes, which are likely to value, among other things, education, personal participation in the political process, and the rule of law. All of these are vital to a healthy democracy. Most importantly of all, market economies put most economic decisions in the hands of individual consumers and producers, rather than in the hands of the government. It is very hard to imagine, particularly in the light of the Soviet experience, political democracy flourishing in an economy where all decisions are taken by the government.

Against the good effects, market economies can produce high levels of economic inequality, which are harmful to democracy. The rich get a better education, better access to information, more chances to influence those in power, and so on. In such a situation, the political equality which has been built into the democratic system becomes more and more meaningless.

To deal with this problem, governments have introduced measures designed to narrow the gap between rich and poor, or at least to prevent it from widening still further. The rich have had money taken from them in higher taxes and the money has been used to give the poor increased support, or welfare benefits. In some countries the rules on political contributions have been tightened up to prevent what amounts to the buying of favours. A huge gap remains, however, and it casts a long shadow over the democratic process.

Contrasting housing in Mumbai (Bombay) in India, where there may be a distance of only a few hundred metres between extreme poverty and wealth.

⑧ Strengths and weaknesses

For most of the last 2000 years, democracy has often been strongly criticized. The great thinkers of their times thought the masses too stupid to rule, and the rich and powerful were too scared of losing their wealth and positions to give them the chance. Yet over the last 100 years, all that has changed. Democracy has been adopted in most of the world's richer countries and continues to spread. These days, people frequently grumble about abuses of democracy or a lack of democracy, but rarely about democracy itself.

Strengths

Democracy gives the people a voice. It allows them to both pick and reject their government. The governments of today's **representative democracies** often wield enormous power between elections. They sometimes behave in a **dictatorial** manner, but in the end they are accountable to the electorate – the people. They know that if they prove brutal or incompetent they can be voted out.

A positive view

'Democracy is the superior form of government, because it is based on a respect for man as a reasonable being.'

(From John F. Kennedy's 1940 college thesis, published as *Why England Slept*)

Democracy could not function without freedom of expression, and freedom of expression can only be guaranteed in a democracy. In a democratic society, people are usually free to do much more than just vote for political representatives. They are also free to learn what they wish to learn, live where they wish to live, work at what they wish to work at.

Freedom implies responsibility, and in a democratic society people are expected to take responsibility for their own lives. Since they have at least some control over the actions of their own government, people cannot wash their hands of responsibility, or claim that they are just following orders. Sharing in the decisions means sharing in the responsibility. In a political sense and perhaps also in a human sense, democracy invites people to grow up.

Democratic countries have tended to be more peaceful, at least when it comes to dealing with other democratic countries. There are several reasons for this, and some of them – such as the possession of nuclear weapons – have nothing to do with democracy. Democratic governments are more used to the idea of solving conflicts through compromise. Their business people have much to lose if disputes and conflicts interrupt trade. Most important of all, democratic politicians are forced to take notice of their citizens' understandable reluctance to risk injury and death.

Democratic governments have continued to fight wars in the **developing world,** but even here public opinion has limited the military options open to them. Since the USA suffered so many casualties in the Vietnam War, the US government has been extremely reluctant to order any military action which might result in the death of American citizens.

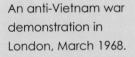

An anti-Vietnam war demonstration in London, March 1968.

Democracy also usually produces wealth and prosperity. **Market economies** and political freedom support and are supported by democracy. Both grow well where an independent **judiciary** enforces the **rule of law**, where information is widely available, where there is no political interference in education, and where creativity is allowed to flourish.

Weaknesses

Democracy also has weaknesses. One already mentioned is the way in which democratic rule can degenerate into the **tyranny** of the majority in situations where basic values are not shared. It is easy to find examples of where this has occurred – Northern Ireland remains the classic example – and equally easy to suggest voting systems and constitutional arrangements which might give the minority community a bigger say in their government. **Proportional representation** would at least ensure that the minority's numbers were reflected in the assembly. The two communities could agree to share power by, for example, making sure that the minority's representatives were always put in charge of some government departments. Of course, if the majority community is unwilling to see its dominant position threatened, any such changes will only have a limited effectiveness.

A cynical view

'Democracy substitutes election by the incompetent many for appointment by the corrupt few.'

(British playwright George Bernard Shaw, in his play *Man and Superman*, 1903)

Another practical weakness lies in democracy's inability to act swiftly and decisively when such action is needed. For example, it is hard to imagine that Stalin's decision in the early 1930s to prepare the Soviet Union for a probable German assault would have ever been taken in a democracy. Stalin sacrificed millions of people with his crash programme of industrialization which was carried out in terrible conditions, but it may well have saved the world from the tyranny of **Nazi** Germany.

Governments elected for a few years are only too aware that they must face the electors in the not-too-distant future. They are often reluctant to take decisions necessary for the country's long-term benefit if they believe that doing so will damage their prospects of winning the next election. Those same governments sometimes borrow and spend large amounts of money on popular projects to help them win the next election, knowing that it will be future governments and generations who will have to pay the bill.

Japanese children from Kyoto hold up a model 'planet of life' at the December 1997 conference on **global warming**. Maintaining popularity with voters can be more important to democratic governments than working for results which may take longer to achieve, such as those agreed at this conference.

45

A final weakness of national democracy – perhaps the most serious it faces – has only become apparent in recent years. Democracy exists within countries at every level, from local clubs to national governments, but it does not often reach out across national boundaries. This was not a problem so long as the important political and economic decisions were taken at national level. However, unfortunately for democracy, that is no longer the case.

A realistic view?

'The tragedy of modern democracies is that they have not yet succeeded in effecting [bringing about] democracy.'

(French political thinker Jacques Maritain, writing in 1940)

⑨ Beyond the nation-state

Since the rise of the nation-state, it has been assumed that governments have the right to exercise authority within national boundaries. When such governments were elected democratically, it meant that the people of those countries had the final say over what happened. Beyond the boundaries of the countries, however, no one held authority. Agreements were reached between countries, but they were not legally binding and there was no international agency to enforce them. The law-abiding, democratic world inside national boundaries and the essentially lawless international arena could co-exist in relative harmony for the simple reason that they rarely came into contact with each other. There was trade between nations, but there were very few truly international businesses.

All this has changed. Over the last 50 years there has been a fast-growing spread of business, culture and communications around the world (globalization). By the end of the 20th century, only 49 of the 100 largest economies on earth were the economies of nations. The other 51 were multinational corporations, businesses operating in several countries. World economic and technological development has created a situation in which the flow of money, goods, services, even culture, across national boundaries has risen in leaps and bounds. These flows, when they are controlled at all, are controlled by multinational corporations, not by governments.

Young women at work in a factory of the multinational Reebok company, outside the Indonesian capital of Jakarta in the 1980s.

Loss of control

As a consequence, democratically elected national governments – and the people who vote for them – are no longer able to control what happens within their own boundaries. Unexpected shifts of the relative value of the currency in different countries can upset a government's economic plans. Businesses can suddenly decide to move their operations from one country to another, leaving unemployment in their wake. The Indian government can do little about the threat which MTV poses to traditional culture. The French government is powerless to stop the French language being invaded by English words, or French culture losing out to American movies and fast food.

If decisions which affect everyone are increasingly being taken beyond the reach of the voter, it would seem logical to extend the voter's reach into the international arena, to create democratic international institutions. Some small progress in this area has been made. The arrest of the former Yugoslav leader Slobodan Milosevic on charges of crimes against humanity, for example, showed that the principle of accountability – holding people responsible for their actions – could reach across international boundaries.

Former Yugoslav President Slobodan Milosevic appears before the UN War Crimes Tribunal at the Hague, July 2001.

Generally speaking, there has been a fierce resistance to democratizing international bodies. Like the richer classes of the 19th century, the richer nations of the 21st are afraid of what the majority might do if given an equal vote.

International democracy?

There are no genuinely democratic international institutions representing the individual people of the world on an equal basis. The United Nations, for example, which was set up in 1945 to promote international peace and cooperation, has majority voting for nations in its General Assembly, but the effectiveness of this is severely limited by the **veto** which five states – the USA, Russia, the UK, France and China – have in the Security Council. Also, small states are subject to all sorts of economic pressure from the larger, richer states.

Flies caught in a web

'What influence do politicians really have in a world of global capitalism? Single-handedly, not much .... Governments are now like flies caught in the intricate web of the market. And voters see their powerlessness. They sense that politicians' hands are tied and that their promises are increasingly empty. They watch politicians dancing to the corporations' tunes .... And so, increasingly, they are turning their backs on politics.'

(Noreena Hertz in *The Silent Takeover*)

International institutions set up to regulate international business are either not **accountable**, like the World Trade Organization, or only marginally democratic, like the European Union. The latter has a powerful appointed Commission, which plans and implements policies, a powerful Council of Ministers composed of national leaders, which decides which policies will be implemented, and a weak democratically elected Parliament, which operates as a debating chamber but cannot make laws. At the beginning of the 21st century, the chances of an elected European government able to take Europe-wide decisions looks remote. The chances of elected global organizations performing a similar role in the world look even bleaker.

49

When it comes to dealing with problems which cross national boundaries, only a few undemocratic international bodies controlled by the richest states, and a large number of corporations accountable only to their shareholders, have any real power or influence.

The consequences of failure

This situation has obvious consequences. The first is that people have begun to realize that their elected governments have much less power and influence than they used to have. In this light, national politics have come to seem increasingly irrelevant to many voters, with the result that both party membership and turn-out at elections have slumped alarmingly in many democratic countries. Some have turned to more direct avenues of protest, others have simply lost interest or given up because they do not think that there is any point in getting involved in politics. Either way, democracy has been the loser.

Greenpeace activists in Sydney, Australia demonstrate against the continued hunting of whales by the Japanese, November 2001.

A second consequence is that the problems thrown up by globalization are either being tackled in the interests of a few or not being tackled effectively. Economic growth has created serious environmental problems, many of which need to be tackled at the international level. **Global warming**, for example, will ultimately effect most people on the planet, but the government of the Maldives, whose country may well be submerged by the rising ocean levels, has no influence over those countries whose industrial pollution is causing the problem. A voluntary agreement to limit this pollution was actually reached at Kyoto in 1997, but in 2001 President Bush announced that the USA (which, with less than 5 per cent of the world's population, is responsible for 25 per cent of the pollution) would not be ratifying the deal. Inside a democratic nation-state it would be impossible for such a small minority to hold the majority hostage in this way.

⑩ So, what is democracy?

In 1863 the US President, Abraham Lincoln, defined democracy as government of the people, by the people, and for the people. This might have been possible in the small city-states of ancient Greece, but in mass societies the most we can hope for is government by the chosen representatives of the people in the interests of the people. These representatives are not required to do what the people – or even a majority of the people – want them to do in any particular situation, but they are expected to carry on the business of government in broad agreement with the people's wishes. If they do not do so, then they can expect to be replaced by others who promise they will.

The recipe for democracy

In order to work, representative democracy requires a system of institutions and rules called a **constitution**. This will lay down – though not always in writing – how and when elections will be conducted, and which of many alternative voting systems will be used. Those elections will usually be contested by parties representing different sets of ideas and interests. All adults will be able to vote.

Other ingredients are also necessary. Without freedom of expression, assembly and association, it would be impossible to have the well-informed debates which allow people to cast a meaningful vote. Without the **rule of law** there is no guarantee that these freedoms will be upheld, that elections will be conducted fairly or that their result will be accepted.

The system will work better, more democratically, in some conditions than others. Democracy will flourish where there are no threats from outside, where armed forces accept the principle of obedience to civil (not

'Democracy is not a static thing. It is an everlasting march.'

(American President Franklin D. Roosevelt, pointing out in a speech in October 1935 that democracy can never be taken for granted, and can always be improved)

military) government, where the mass of the people have long agreed it is the only acceptable way to run things, where important political and religious values are shared, and where there is a rough measure of economic equality. It will struggle to survive where enemies threaten, where armed forces have influence over civil affairs, where a significant number of people still believe there is an alternative, where important values are not shared, or where there is a wide degree of economic inequality.

The **capitalist**, free **market economy** both encourages democracy by decentralizing decision-making and undermines it by promoting inequality. Some freedoms are also two-edged. The freedom to support a party of your choice financially is a good example. An individual voter handing over a few pounds is contributing to the democratic process; a corporation handing over millions is trying to bribe a future government, to distort the democratic process.

A huge crowd in the Czechoslovak capital Prague celebrates the fall of communism and the country's imminent return to democracy in November 1989. In 1993 Czechoslovakia peacefully split into two states – the Czech Republic and Slovakia.

Are you living in a democracy?

So how can you tell if you are living in a democracy? Imagine a country with a long-established democratic constitution, well-organized parties, an educated population, a long history of respect for the rule of law. In this country the media is dominated by a few companies, the major parties have very similar policies, and there is a growing gap between rich and poor. Is it a democracy?

A matter of degree

'Democracy is a matter of degree. Some countries are more democratic than others. But none is perhaps very democratic, if any high standard of democracy is applied. Mass democracy is a difficult and hitherto largely uncharted territory, and we should be nearer the mark, and should have a far more convincing slogan, if we spoke of the need, not to defend democracy, but to create it.'

(The English historian E.H. Carr, arguing that modern society still has some way to go to create a true democracy)

Our imaginary country could be either the USA or the UK, both of which like to think of themselves as democracies. Some parts of the description support that view, other parts raise doubts. It is perhaps more useful to think of democracy as a job that is far from finished, to remember how much less democratic these two countries were 100 years ago, and to imagine how much more democratic they might make themselves in the future. Many people would consider six out of ten a fair score for the beginning of the 21st century.

The prospects

Will this score rise? Some observers are optimistic. They point out how many countries have made the transition from dictatorship to democracy, particularly in the last few decades. Others are pessimistic. They stress the limited nature of the democracies which now exist, and the new threat posed by the growing influence of multinational corporations which are not politically **accountable**. They fear that democracy is becoming all form and no substance.

Time will tell. Perhaps the best clue is offered by the prehistoric hunters we encountered in Chapter 2 as they sat round their fire, discussing when they were going to hunt the next day. They instinctively knew that using everyone's knowledge and experience would give them a better chance of eating tomorrow. Ten thousand years later, democracy still offers the best chance of fulfilling the promise of every human being.

Timeline

c. 510–50 BC	Roman Republic
c. 507–321 BC	Greek city-states such as Athens adopt a limited form of democracy
c. 930–1230	Icelandic Althing
1215	Magna Carta is signed at Runnymede between King John and the English barons
c. 1300	Assemblies called by Edward I grow into the English **Parliament**
c. 1450	Representative assembly in Sweden
1642–49	English **civil war**
1647	Putney Debates on the future government of England and Wales
1649	Execution of King Charles I
1688	The Glorious Revolution in England and Wales
1776	Declaration of Independence in the USA
1788	Adoption of the US **Constitution**
1789–94	**French Revolution**
1793	New French constitution (briefly) gives vote to all men
1832	First Parliamentary Reform Act in the UK gives vote to small landowners and some tenant farmers
1856	Australia introduces **secret ballot**
1861–65	US civil war
1867	Second Parliamentary Reform Act in the UK gives the vote to all male householders in towns and more tenant farmers
1872	UK introduces secret ballot
1884	USA introduces secret ballot
	Third Parliamentary Reform Act in the UK gives vote to all male householders
1893	New Zealand becomes the first country to give women the vote
1902	Australian women get the vote
1906	Finland becomes the first European country to give women the vote
1914–18	World War I

1917	Russian Revolution
1918	All men, and all women over 30 are given the vote in the UK
1920	All women in the USA given the vote
1922	Fascism, the dictatorial system known for its aggressive nationalism, comes to power in Italy
1928	All women over 21 given the vote in the UK
1933	**Nazism** comes to power in Germany
1939–45	World War II – fascism and Nazism defeated
***c.* 1947–87**	The **Cold War**
1957–65	Civil rights movement in the USA tries to enforce African Americans' voting rights
1968	Czechoslovakia's moves toward democracy are crushed by Soviet tanks
	Civil rights movement against **tyranny** of majority begins in Northern Ireland
1973	Chilean democracy is crushed by the US-supported Chilean Army
1978–79	Students and others put up posters on Democracy Wall in Beijing
1983	Military rule gives way to democracy in Argentina
1989	Pro-democracy protests in Beijing's Tiananmen Square are crushed
1989–91	Fall of **communism** in Europe
1990	Aung San Suu Kyi's National League for Democracy wins 80% of seats in Burma's national election, but its victory is not recognized by the military government
1992	Algerian elections cancelled when Islamic fundamentalists seem certain to win
1994	African National Congress wins first democratic elections in South Africa
2000	George W. Bush elected US **president** with fewer votes than opponent Al Gore

Further reading

Democracy, Nathaniel Harris (Hodder Wayland, 2001)
What do we Mean by Equal Rights? (Watts, 2002)
What do we Mean by Freedom of Speech? (Watts, 2002)

Sources

Anthony Arblaster, *Democracy* (Open University Press, 1994)
Robert Alan Dahl, *On Democracy* (Yale University Press, 1998)
Noreena Hertz, *The Silent Takeover* (William Heinemann, 2001)

Films and TV

The Candidate (1972, directed by Michael Ritchie, starring Robert
   Redford)
Fame is the Spur (1946, directed by Roy Boulting, starring
   Michael Redgrave)
All the President's Men (1976, directed by Alan J. Pakula, starring
   Dustin Hoffman and Robert Redford)
The West Wing (2000–, TV series set in the office of the US
   president)
Yes, Minister and *Yes, Prime Minister* (1980s comedy TV series set
   in the British House of Commons)

Websites

The Democracy Network (US): www.dnet.org/
Political Science Resources: www.psr.keele.ac.uk/
Politics Direct: www.politicsdirect.com/
Parliamentary Reform 1750–1900:
   www.spartacus.schoolnet.co.uk/PRparliament.htm
USAID: Democracy Around the World: www.usaid.gov/democracy/
International Centre for Human Rights and Democratic
   Development: www.ichrdd.ca/flash.html
Elections Around the World: www.electionworld.org/

Some key people in the history of democracy

Susan B. Anthony (1820–1906) was originally active in the American anti-slavery and temperance (anti-alcohol) movements, but from the 1850s was primarily concerned with winning the vote for women. In 1869 she became leader of the National American Woman Suffrage (right to vote) Association, and in 1904 she organized the International Woman Suffrage Alliance in Berlin.

Aung San Suu Kyi (1945–) co-founded and became leader of Burma's National League for Democracy (NLD) in 1988. In the run-up to the 1990 elections she was placed under house arrest and not allowed to stand. The NLD won 80% of the seats but its victory was not recognized by the military government. Aung San Suu Kyi's belief in democracy and non-violence won her the Nobel Peace Prize in 1991, but ten years later Burma was still ruled by a military **dictatorship**.

Mikhail Gorbachev (1931–) served as General Secretary of the Soviet **Communist** Party from 1985 to 1991, and as President of the Soviet Union from 1988 to 1991. He brought an end to the **Cold War** and introduced major reforms of the Soviet political and economic system. By ending the communist monopoly of power and encouraging more open government, he created the conditions for a transition to democracy in both the Soviet Union and its former junior partners in eastern Europe.

Václav Havel (1936–), a Czech playwright, became a spokesman for human rights and pro-democracy groups in Czechoslovakia in the 1970s. Twice imprisoned, he founded the Civic Reform group on his second release in 1989, and was prominent in the campaign for political change which culminated later that year in Czechoslovakia's peaceful transition from communism to democracy, the so-called Velvet Revolution. He became **President**, first of Czechoslovakia, then of the Czech Republic, after Czechoslovakia split into the Czech Republic and Slovakia in 1993.

59

Thomas Jefferson (1743–1826) was primarily responsible for drafting the American Declaration of Independence. During discussions on the new state's **constitution**, his arguments in favour of more democracy were highly influential. He stressed the need for a clear separation of powers between the different arms of government, and for a decentralized **federal** system.

Martin Luther King (1929–68) led the civil rights movement in the American South, beginning with the Montgomery bus boycott in 1955–56, until his assassination in Memphis. His early efforts were directed towards ending racial segregation, and after proving successful in this regard he turned his attention to African American voting rights. His 1965 campaign resulted in a Voting Rights Bill which guaranteed African Americans both the right to vote and the freedom to do so.

Nelson Mandela (1918–) was active in South Africa's African National Congress (ANC) from the 1940s. His campaign against white rule (**apartheid**) resulted in his imprisonment in 1964. On his release in 1990 he resumed leadership of the ANC and conducted the negotiations with whites which led to majority rule. In 1994 he was elected President of South Africa.

Emmeline Pankhurst (1858–1928) led the women's suffrage movement in Britain. She founded the Women's Social and Political Union in 1903, and for the next 11 years, until the outbreak of World War I, she and her elder daughter Christabel led a mass campaign for the women's vote which involved the imprisonment of thousands and the destruction of property.

Socrates (*c.* 470–399 BC) was one of the most significant of the Greek **philosophers**. He was the teacher of *Plato* (*c.* 429–347 BC), whose writings contained many of the ideas of Socrates. Plato in turn was a teacher of *Aristotle* (*c.* 384–322 BC), who became tutor to Alexander the Great and wrote a huge quantity of works on a vast range of subjects, from biology to politics and poetry.

Glossary

accountable having to explain and justify decisions and actions

apartheid system of enforced racial segregation in South Africa from 1948 to 1991

Cabinet group appointed by president or prime minister, composed of government department heads

capitalism economic system in which the production and distribution of goods depend on private wealth and profit-making

civil war war between different groups in one country

Cold War name given to the hostility that existed between the capitalist and communist worlds between about 1947 and the late 1980s

communism originally an extreme form of socialism, in which property is held communally (in common) rather than individually. The Russian Bolsheviks, who seized power in the second Russian Revolution of 1917, renamed themselves the Russian Communist Party. The term communism became associated with the dictatorial state and system of economic planning which was created in the Soviet Union during the 1920s and 30s.

constitution in politics, the way a country is set up to safeguard its fundamental principles

corruption immoral practices like bribery and fraud

developing world countries in Africa, Asia and Latin America with underdeveloped economies

dictatorship government by an individual (called a dictator) or a small group that does not allow the mass of the people to have any say in their government

executive in government, the individual or body which has the duty of introducing and enforcing new measures and laws

federal state (or federation) country made up of several states or provinces. Some powers are exercised at the central or federal level, others at the state or provincial level.

French Revolution political upsurge in France which developed into a full-scale assault on the upper classes. It ended with the 1793–94 reign of terror in which the King and many aristocrats were executed.

global warming the gradual warming of Earth's atmosphere, which is mostly caused by rising levels of carbon dioxide (also called the Greenhouse Effect). The increased burning of fossil fuels (as, for example, in cars) and the accelerating destruction of the planet's forests are the main source of these rising levels.

House of Lords upper house of the British Parliament

judiciary those responsible for administering and upholding the legal system

legislature law-making (legislative) assembly

market economy economy in which decisions are taken by buyers and sellers in a free market

monarchy government headed by a monarch (king, queen, emperor, etc.), who usually inherits the position from his or her father or mother

Nazi abbreviation (in German) for Hitler's National Socialist Party, which ruled Germany between 1933 and 1945

parliament legislative assembly which has been at least partly elected

philosopher thinker about life

presidency in the USA, the executive arm of government. In many countries the president is the supreme authority.

proportional representation (PR) voting system which tries to ensure that the number of votes cast for each party is accurately reflected in the number of seats each party wins

Protestantism form of Christianity which split off from the Catholic church in the 16th century

representative democracy system in which people elect representatives to take decisions for them

rule of law situation in which the law of the country is obeyed by all, including those in government and the armed services

secret ballot system in which no one knows how any particular person votes

sovereignty power

tyranny harsh and undemocratic rule

undemocratic not taking account of the electorate's wishes

unitary state state in which the central government has complete authority

veto a right to reject a decision or proposal made by a law-making body

Index